AF261522

Personification

of

Entelechy

A book of poems by

Stacy Schlagel

ISBN 978-1-7330579-3-6

Sivad Publishing
PO Box 62328
Houston, TX 77205

Printed in USA by Ingram Spark

First printing, July 2020

Acknowledgments

First off, I would like to thank my good Lord and Savior Jesus Christ, and my brilliant parents, for instilling a dogged determination in me to never give up and always pursue my dreams. I would also like to personally thank my many, many supportive girlfriends for pushing me to write and become published. Thank you to my first cousin, Tamatha Davis, who published me and made my dreams come true. Thanks to my son, Zachary, for teaching me the true meaning of sacrificial love. Lastly, thanks to my dedicated and loyal husband who has stuck by my side and supported me in any and every endeavor I choose to embark upon. I love you all so very much, and thank you again!

Preface

Dear Reader,

We live in such a fast-paced society where we rarely have time to be introspective, let alone share our intrinsic ideas with others. My hope is to inspire others to "feel", at the very least, something other than the chaos that is going on around us, often leaving us feeling depleted, vexed or objectified.

-Stacy Elizabeth Schlagel

Table of Contents

Inspiration

"Moonlight Lovers"

You see me beneath the trees

On a golden dewy autumn night

Lovers quarrel and they fight

Sadness brings her to her knees

He is also melancholy

As both lovers deem to please

She sighs

He walks out of sight

Both hearts began to break

Both tremor and violently shake

Making their way back to the moonlight

They hold an intoxicating embrace

She missed his beautiful face

He took her hand, as they began

LIFE

Together, forever

Under the golden moonlight

                              "Pretty Face"

So they think I'm merely a pretty face

A stereotype I can't seem to escape

As I scream from within

WAIT, I have so many talents

While I stay modest

And inwardly focused

Those that love me the most

 See my soul

They judge me not

Knowing I will quickly pop off

What everyone needs to discover

Please don't judge a book by its cover

"Take Me"

Pink Peonies on bending knees

I ask thee

Oh, please choose me

My lovely lady

A beautiful blue butterfly, flying high

Take my hand, or I shall surely die

I love thee now until forever

Into every cosmos, universe, and thereafter

Without you I'm merely a fallen disaster

An exploded heart

Oh please my beautiful butterfly,say yes, until death us do part.

My tenderness replies with tears in her eyes

Oh my

Yes, I surely do take thee

My beautiful butterfly, I promise to make you smile

Your most beautiful smile, daily

You just made me the happiest man in history!

"What is This Life for?"

How did we get here, how will all this end?

Those are questions only HE can answer

My curious and benevolent friend

Let's open our hearts, minds and eyes, and realize

HE is in ultimate control

We are spinning on a ball in wide open space

What is this life for?

It's unconditional love, not malice or hate

My heart is wide open for love from all mankind:

The creative and restless genius

The entrepreneur always seeking more

The athlete who needs to perform

The doctors that try to save us all

The leaders with no clue

Teachers who don't know what to do

Children who want to play

The poor man who is afraid

And the homeless who can't seem to bear one more day...

We cannot escape the unending pain

Let's rejoice in this day and choose to love not hate

Calm your minds and open your hearts

HE is in control, so throw fear out

Love your neighbor

There is no doubt, that is what this life is about

In the end, let's hope we all meet again

In a majestic place, called heaven

"Make Lemonade"

When life gives you lemons

Don't complain

Make lemonade

Compete only with yourself, and do the very best you
can do

Let others' greatness inspire you

Jealousy, a wasted emotion, can surely drag your down

Stand up and be proud

Thank God for all your blessings

This is the key to happiness, you see

Keep your head up, and focus on the best you can be

Life is a journey, a series of ups and downs

Don't pout

Stand up and be proud

Learn from your mistakes; don't get stuck in your past

Make the happy memories last

Life is a game you can most definitely master

Let gratitude and love be your oyster

"Quarantine and Covid-19"

My sweet family and supportive friends

I never knew how much I needed you, until you were not around

I never knew how weak I was, until I was no longer strong

The piercing pain I feel is literally insane

The sun is out many days, but for me, it can feel like rain

I've never been so lonely in my life, with the absence of your love and affection

I yearn for togetherness and our close connection

My heart bleeds for love more and more with each passing day; however, my spirit of gratitude keeps me from the everyday mundane.

More than ever I thought possible, what would it take to feel safe

I'm learning to find imminent strength in my newfound weakness,

And to tell myself, it will all be okay

As some say, this is all a hoax

I plead with them, this is absolutely no joke

I want to see my family's faces, I yearn for their embraces

I miss my friends so much it hurts, as the tears occasionally spurt

The little girl inside me, who desperately needs love,

Will find a way to be strong again, with the help and enveloping love from above

To all my sweet family and my supportive friends, I love you

And also, I miss you too

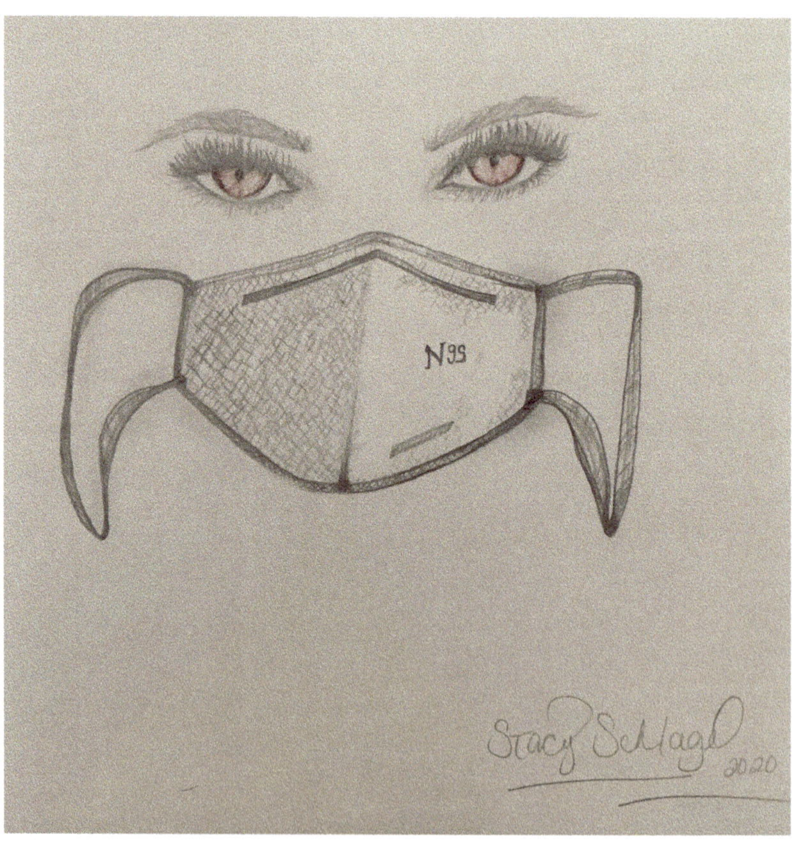

"My Most Precious Gift"

Being a mommy has changed my life for the better

Even though most days I can't think because of all the chatter

My husband frequently asking, what in the heck is the matter?

I can't believe God has trusted me with such an amazing gift

So unbelievably challenging, I must admit

Having my baby live inside me was a unique experience

Some days I miss it

Although other days I throw my hands up and want to quit

I will never forget

My baby, Zachary, is my most precious gift

"Stepford Wife"

When you are walking down the aisle, you are seeing
fairytales and rainbows

Not noisy kids throwing twigs

You absolutely do not know

The impact of this big decision

Who am I, merely a Stepford wife?

He scolds, he folds

This is how the cookie crumbles

Women, find your own voice

It's a matter of CHOICE

Be humble, do not stumble

Make the time to let your OWN light shine

Your family will surely appreciate you

You are not a Stepford wife

Oh how Divine

Friends & Family

                              "Family Tree"

To my family,

Everyone has done a many great things

If you devoted your life to our country

You are self-made

Musically inclined

Harvard Grads

Great moms and dads

Doctors, authors, artists, professors, politicians,
mathematicians

The list is endless

I'm thankful for your love

A true gift from above

Our family tree is astounding

At times bewildering

Often unyielding

However, I'm thankful for thee

Thank you for loving and inspiring me

My family tree

"Baby Brother"

Baby brother

I thought I was your mother

I've taken care of you since you were two

Stubborn and independent

With uncanny resistance

You could barely walk, talk, or eat off of a plate

Never failing to negotiate

You put on those skates

I said, "Baby, please wait"

We were inseparable through the years

Sharing our joys, hopes, and fears

I had so much fun living life with you

You are now all grown up, and a physician too

Baby brother, I love you

"Thru Covid"

Doctor

My Personal Physician

Thank you for being there for me through Covid

What life-altering moments

Without you, I would not have been able to hack it

I'd probably be in a straitjacket

Thanks for giving my brother those masks

I enjoyed getting to know you, man

You helped me to become a better person

                              "My Alpha Male"

Born to lead and overachieve

At times he drives me absolutely crazy

Women do indeed submit

He intrinsically knows this

Has innate and great wit, what a gift

He will do "big things" one day

Not getting his own way

Throws a fit, he never quits

Mom takes deep breaths to stay sane

Refusing to let him have his own way

Rule breaker

Mover and a shaker

Mom's unconditional love, gives him lots of hugs

He demands; mom doesn't hover

Desires independence

Defiant and obstinate

Deeply empathetic and giving

Often says, "Sharing is caring"

Life with him can be both Heaven on Earth,

But also a complete hell

Mostly, rather swell

I will ALWAYS wish him well

My little alpha male

           "Lee Lee"

She is oh so friendly

So chic

Fancy free

A rich hippy

My love for this beauty runs deep

She has really helped me

Be a better mom, person, friend

We have a bond

That will never be broken

She will be right by my side

My bestie

For life

"Nicole"

I love her sweet soul

Don't let her fool you,

She is in control

If we are dying laughing or crying

Or anything in between

Our chemistry

Is mesmerizing

I'm so blessed God brought

Her into my life

My ride or die

"Sonya"

How will I start this?

She is intense

Determined

Worked in the White House

A powerhouse, no doubt

My loyal and trustworthy friend

Proclivity towards strength

Rarely showing weakness

She lets her guard down with me

I consider myself lucky

Truly unique and one of my besties

I'm fiercely protective of this beauty

She will always mean

So very much to me

"Trudy Madan"

When you walked into my life

I thought you were drop dead gorgeous

Little did I know we would reconnect through Covid?

The reason we were brought together, I don't care

Just as long as you are there

Laughing, crying, challenging one another in close moments

When I see you, I see your soul

As I see my own

Strong, yet sensitive

Open yet closed

Always searching for more

We both are hot and cold

I'm so happy I have you

in my life baby girl

You and I, we always keep it real

I admire and appreciate you

So much, you have no clue

My love for you will always be

Deep and true

"Lindsay"

What a treat

She will let you know what she really thinks

So very special to me

She keeps me dying laughing

Her eyes are hypnotizing

She really challenges me

Sensitive yet strong

We have that in common

I love my baby girl

She keeps it real

My sweet friend

Until the end

"Jolie"

Jolie

Quite candid

Penchant for science

Brilliant

Chooses to keep this hidden

Together our souls radiate with joy

I see her for who she really is

At times, rather coy

Funny how life gives you a friend

You instantly connect with,

And the connection is resilient

My one wish in friendship, I'm thankful for this

My friend, Jolie

"My True Ride or Die"

Hubby!

Thanks for putting up with me

I'm high maintenance and demanding

You often compliment me

Mentioning

But dreamy and rather enchanting

What would you do without me, baby?

I'm so lucky to be your wifey

You arc incredibly amazing!

And oh so sweet

Thank you for spoiling me and sweeping me off my feet

As we navigate this thing called life

There is no place I'd rather be

 Except right by your side

My True Ride or Die

"Sisters"

Sisters feud

So unattractive, so rude?

I exclaim, make your way to the sunlight!

Do what is right!

How crude

Another royal fight

Sister for this

Some get sued

I blow you a kiss

Let you off lightly not in the blissful mood

Choosing to keep my sovereignty

Sweeping it under the rug,

Not Dragging my name

through the mud

Until the next trifling thud

Sisters genuinely hug,

And kindly choose LOVE

Doing what is right,

Making their way

to the sunlight

Christian

"I'm Forgiven"

Heaven's Water Flows

I see angels

Royal blood

Save us from the flood

Your unconditional love

I know I'm forgiven

You rose from the dead

Made me a better man

Thank you again, I'm forgiven

And part of your highborn plan

Guilt plagues, waters rage

I'm undeserving, of anything holy

I've sinned, and I'm forgiven

My heart beats, I'm brought to my knees

Jesus save me, love me, hug me, hold me

You know me, please show me

Guilt plagues, waters rage

As you show me the way

My sin

Is forgiven

"Heaven's Fire"

Thank you for loving the sinner that I am

Your righteous right hand

Keeps me from sin

And in your Perfect Plan

Please shine your bright light on our great land

Heaven's Angels sing to me

Oh God, I'm undeserving

Please God, forgive me

Heaven's Fire

Quench my humanly desire

As I aspire

To be a better person

Your humble servant

"His Sacrifice"

I was blind, hard to find

Searching for my soul

I lied, then cried

Meadows glow

He died, His sacrifice

He is mighty,

His glory, He holds me

You reap what you sow

My fight is sin from within

Waters flow

I confess

I labor, my Savior, give me favor

Meadows glow, waters flow

Now I'm alive, YOUR sacrifice

Your holiness,

Thank you, Jesus

"He Was Crowned"

The ground began to shake

What a glorious name

Heaven came down

He was crowned

As the people began to shout

Jesus, Jesus

As it began to rain

Jesus took our pain

Holy Water

You are our Father

Jesus, Jesus

The Sermon on the Mount

The people began to shout

He was crowned

Jesus, Jesus, Jesus, Jesus

The righteous living were glorified

He died to save our lives

The righteous dead were resurrected

We all held hands

As Earth became Heaven

Jesus, Jesus,

Jesus, Jesus

Holy Water

You are our Father

One day soon

We will be a-new with you

 In Heaven

"My Sweet Jesus"

Here I am again on my knees

Begging for peace

This world's misery

So stifling

Jesus

Please shine your light on me

This fight

Bigger than we know

You do not condone

The pain in my soul

Jesus, you make me whole

My faith is not in this world

My faith is in you, JESUS

Sweet Jesus

Your presence

Feels like heaven

With you sweet Jesus

I have joy

I have peace

Oh boy

Thank you sweet Jesus

I have faith

Through my mistakes

I give you my ALL

Lord, with you I will not fall

Thank you, Jesus

My sweet Jesus

About the Author

Stacy Elizabeth Schlagel is an author, philanthropist, mother and homemaker. Stacy is also a songwriter, music producer, plus owner and operator of Regal Recordings. She is passionate about writing, science, interior design, cooking and travel. She was born in Tucson, Arizona on April 8 to two adoring parents, who met in a calculus class in college. The family lived in Arizona for two years after Stacy's birth. They later moved to Austin, Texas, where she would spend her early childhood. Stacy was a precocious and quick-witted child with a keen sense of justice. She made friends quickly. Her kindergarten teacher would describe her in this way, *"She thinks she is everyone's mommy."*

Stacy's dad is a retired missile command officer in the U.S. Air Force, and her mom is a retired trigonometry and calculus high school educator. They both instilled in Stacy the value of hard work, honesty, giving back to your community and competing only with oneself.

Stacy was in her first published magazine as a model at eight years old. She was also in ballet and cheerleading; however, what she loved most was zip-lining and playing outside most of the day with the neighborhood children. During her adolescent years, she developed a strong desire to express herself through creative writing, and did so often rapidly advancing above grade level in language arts, mathematics, and science, which she still enjoys very much to this day.

As a teenager, she continued to model, was a cheerleader, and became involved in beauty competitions, which all have prepared her for life. Upon entering college at the University of Texas/San Antonio campus, Stacy decided to delve into web design. She created her own HTML coding plus Photoshop, and quickly started her own web design business that she owned and operated until she graduated. She also managed to graduate from college with honors and with a background in teaching and law.

Today Stacy is married to David Allen Schlagel, who owns and operates the Natural Resource Consortium. They have one young son named Zachary who is precocious and strong willed, while empathetic and kind. She has an older sister who is a kindergarten educator and a younger brother who is a physician. The Schlagel family strongly believes in giving back to their community and living a Godly life full of learning, new experiences and adventure. Stacy says, *"Learn from your past, live for today, plan for your future, and make every day count."*

Photos with Friends & Family

"Sharing experiences with my family and friends is the most gratifying and important part of my life!"
-Stacy Elizabeth Schlagel

(Left to Right)
Stacy Schlagel & son, Zachary Schlagel
Zachary Schlagel & husband, Dave Schlagel
Zachary Schlagel

(Left to Right)
Schlagel Family
Schlagel Family
Stacy and Zachary Schlagel

(Left to Right)
Stacy Schlagel, mother, Sheila Lloyd, and sister, Andrea Wiatrek
Stacy Schlagel
Stacy Schlagel and Tamatha A. Davis, first cousin and book
publisher

(Left to Right)
Nicole McClane, Stacy Schlagel and Lindsay Bolner
Rocio Heller, Stacy Schlagel, Amy Buenabenta, Xitlalt Salazar, Trudy Madan, and Klye Munoz
Stacy Schlagel, Xitlalt Salazar, and Henry De La Pez

(Left to Right)
Stacy Schlagel and Nicole McClane
Rocio Heller, Stacy Schlagel and Nicole McClane
Sonya Williams and Stacy Schlagel

(Left to Right)
Zachary Schlagel
Lee Lee and Stacy Schlagel